Little Pebble

T0052269

MIGHTY
MILITARY MACHINES

Humvees

A 4D BOOK

by Matt Scheff

PEBBLE
a capstone imprint

Little Pebble is published by Pebble
1710 Roe Crest Drive, North Mankato,
Minnesota 56003
www.mycapstone.com

Library of Congress Cataloging-in-Publication Data
Library of Congress Cataloging-in-Publication data is available from the Library of Congress website.

ISBN 978-1-9771-0109-9 (hardcover)
ISBN 978-1-9771-0115-0 (paperback)
ISBN 978-1-9771-0121-1 (eBook PDF)

Editorial Credits
Marissa Kirkman, editor; Heidi Thompson, designer;
Jo Miller, media researcher; Tori Abraham, production specialist

Photo Credits
iStockphoto: Rockfinder, 5; U.S. Air Force photo by Airman 1st Class Kaleb Snay, 17, Staff Sgt. Matthew Smith, 11; U.S. Air National Guard photo by Master Sgt. Matt Hecht, 9; U.S. Army National Guard photo by Sgt. Adrian Borunda, 19, Staff Sgt. Brian A. Barbour, 21; U.S. Army photo by Spc John Russell, cover, Visual Information Specialist Paolo Bovo, 13; U.S. Marine Corps Combat Camera photo by Lance Cpl. Eryn L. Edelman, 15, U.S. Marine Corps photo by Lance Cpl. Amy Phan, 7
Design Elements: Shutterstock: Zerbor

This is a Capstone 4D book!

Want fun videos that go with this book?

Just visit www.capstone4d.com

Use this password

humvees.01099

Printed in the United States 5051

Table of Contents

What is a Humvee? 4

Humvees in Action 6

Humvee Parts 14

Glossary 22
Read More 23
Internet Sites 23
Critical Thinking Questions . . 24
Index 24

What is a Humvee?

Zoom!

A truck speeds over the land.

It is a Humvee.

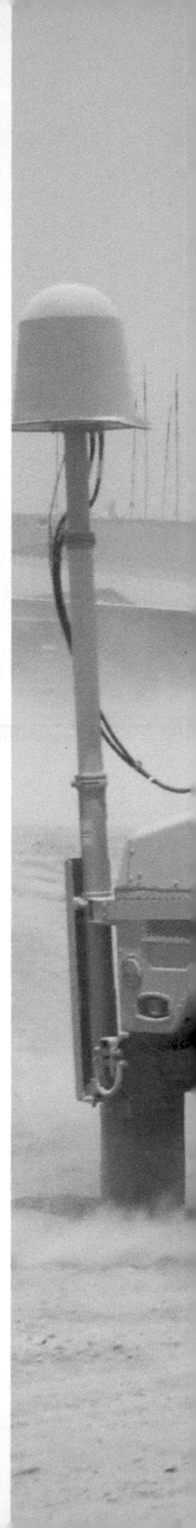

TP 40

This Humvee helps people.

It takes them to safety.

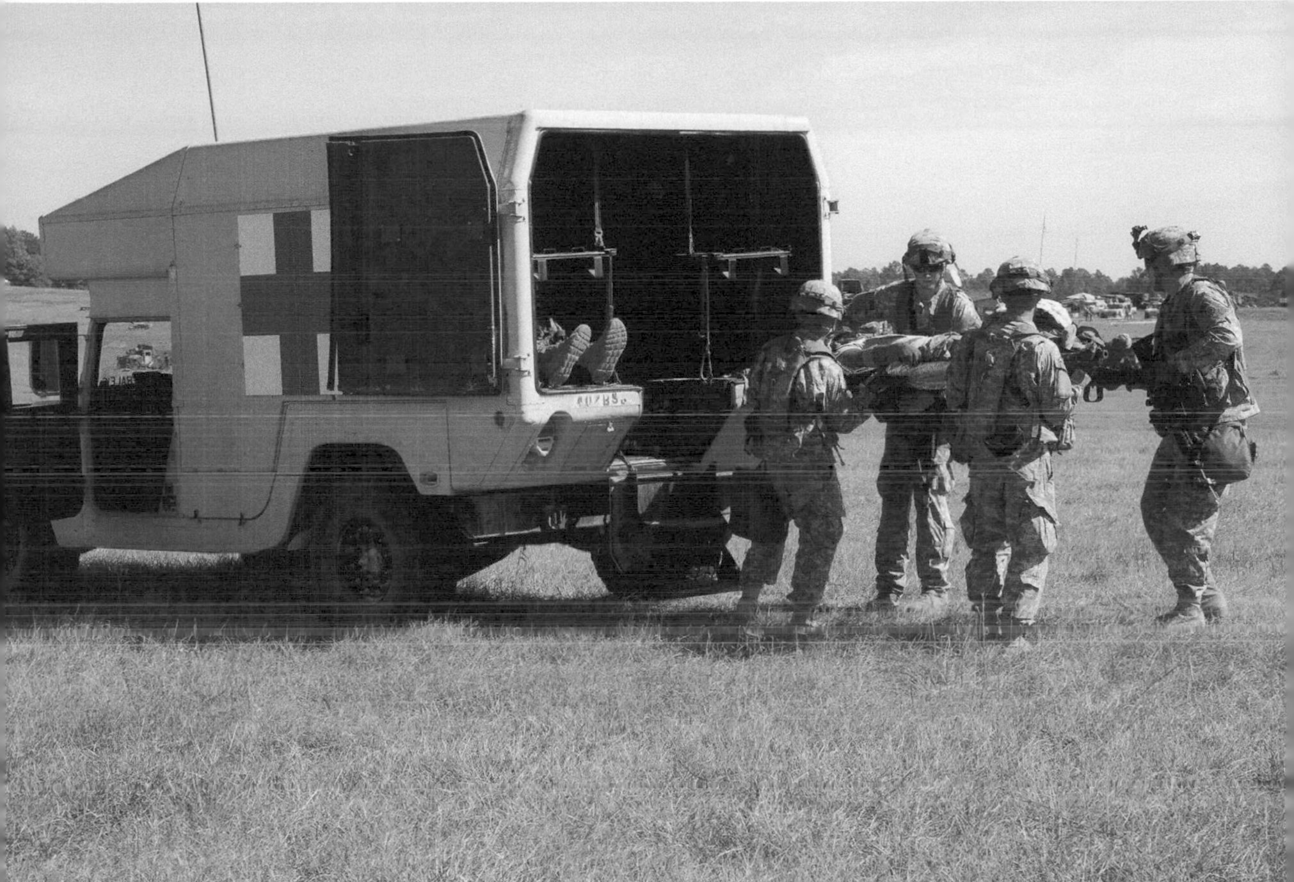

Look up!

This Humvee drops

from a plane!

Humvee Parts

Humvees have big tires.

The tires have deep tread.

They roll over the land.

TIE-DOWN
tread

Bang! Boom!

Humvees have big guns.

They have missiles too.

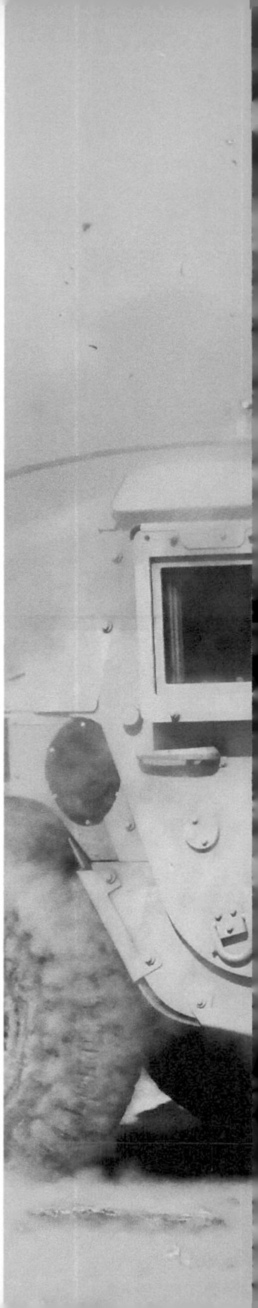

D34
IP40

Glossary

army—a group of soldiers trained to fight on land

cargo—objects carried by a ship, aircraft, or other vehicle

engine—a machine that makes the power needed to move something

missile—an explosive weapon that is thrown or shot at a distant target

soldier—a person who is in the military

tread—the bumps and grooves on a vehicle's tire that help the tire grip the land or road

Read More

Doeden, Matt. *The U.S. Army.* The U.S. Military Branches. North Mankato, Minn.: Capstone Press, 2018.

Graubart, Norman D. *Armored Trucks.* Giants on the Road. New York: PowerKids Press, 2015.

Willis, John. *Humvees.* Mighty Military Machines. New York: AV2 by Weigl, 2017.

Internet Sites

Use FactHound to find Internet sites related to this book.

Visit *www.facthound.com*
Just type in 9781977101099 and go.

Critical Thinking Questions

1. Which part gives a Humvee its power?
2. What do soldiers use Humvees for?
3. How does the deep tread on the tires help the Humvee?

Index

army, 6
cargo, 6
engines, 16
guns, 18
missiles, 18
planes, 12
soldiers, 8, 20
tires, 14
tread, 14
trucks, 4, 6, 8, 16